A COLORFUL BOUQUET OF SAINTS

A GUIDE TO THE MARONITE HERITAGE
THROUGH RELIGIOUS ART IN
St. John Maron Church
BUFFALO, NEW YORK

REV. GEORGES Y. EL-KHALLI
MARTIN F. EDERER

Imprimatur: The Most Revered Stephen Hector Doueihi, S.T.D.
Eparch (Bishop) of the Eparchy of Saint Maron of Brooklyn

Murals and Stained Glass Illustrations:
Courtesy of St. John Maron Maronite Church, Williamsville,
New York

Cover design: Magdi Mushriqui

Icon credit: Tim Martin

Stained Glass credit: Willet Stained Glass Studios

ISBN: 1-893757-29-3

UPC CODE 9 781893 757295

Printed in the United States of America

E.T. NEDDER Publishing
PMB # 299
9121 East Tanque Verde, Suite 105
Tucson, AZ 85749-8390

Table of Contents

Acknowledgments   ii

Dedication   iii

Preface of Bishop Stephen Hector Doueihi   iv

Foreword   vi

Part I   Introduction   1

Part II   Eastern and Western Catholic Churches   5

Part III   Identity of the Maronite Church   9

Part IV   A Brief History of Our Parish   17

Part V   Overview of the New Artwork   21

Part VI   The Lives of the Saints:

            (A) Murals   27

            (B) Stained Glass Windows   41

Conclusion   77

Exemplary Contributors   79

Appendix: Generous Sponsors

Acknowledgments

This project owes its existence to many individuals who through their suggestions and encouragement have helped the process of its completion.

We would like to thank the following:

Our dear shepherd, His Excellency Bishop Stephen Hector Doueihi, S.T.D., Eparch of Saint Maron of Brooklyn who, in spite of his busy schedule, took time to provide the preface. His great encouragement, constructive comments and precious opinion brought this work to fruition. We are indebted to him for his guidance, inspiration and approval for this book.

Our dear friend, the shepherd of the Diocese of Buffalo, His Excellency Bishop Henry Mansell, D.D., whose solicitude for the Maronites in Western New York, and whose encouragement and support strengthened our commitment to complete it. We are also grateful for his gracious assistance in promoting this work in his Diocese. Chorbishop Seely J. Beggiani, S.T.D., the rector of the Maronite Seminary in Washington D.C., who through his expertise provided invaluable feedback and reviewed the doctrinal content of this book.

A word of gratitude goes to Dr. Felix Labaki, who helped editing and proofreading the final draft; to Mrs. Elizabeth Khangi-Gates for facilitating computer complexities in adjusting text and picture, and for formatting the final production of the text; and to Mr. Kamal Aboujaoude and Mr. Ernest T. Nedder for their publishing and printing advice.

A word of gratitude is owed to the families who donated the icons, the transoms and the windows; to the families who committed their support to the printing of this book; to the parishioners who contributed to the renovation of our Church; to Mr. Tim Martin, who ornamented the sanctuary of our church with his artistic talent; and to Willet Stained Glass Studios, which produced the new windows.

Dedication

On the occasion of celebrating the Centennial of St. John Maron parish community we wish to dedicate this book to the priests who founded, and for one hundred years served, as pastors or assistant pastors, the altar of St. John Maron and who spiritually nourished the flock of St. Maron in the Buffalo area. They are listed alphabetically as follows:

Rev. Maroun Abi-Nader

Rev. Simon Acle

Rev. George Aziz

Msgr. Nemat-Allah Chemaly

Rev. Fouad El-Hage (presently bishop Youhanna El-Hage)

Rev. Paul Hage

Msgr. Joseph D. Joseph

Rev. Silwanus Joudy

Rev. Philip Nagem

Rev. Norman S. Peter

Rev. Peter F. Sfeir

Msgr. Francis Shemalie

Rev. Antoun A. Zoghby

We also wish to dedicate this book to the parents and grandparents who passed on and who provided us with a great heritage, and afforded us this spiritual home.

Finally, we dedicate this book to all the parishioners who supported St. John Maron parish community for the last one hundred years.

Preface

Office of the Bishop
EPARCHY OF SAINT MARON
OF BROOKLYN
109 Remsen Street
Brooklyn, New York 11201
Tel: (718) 237-9913
Fax: (718) 243-0444

This *"Colorful Bouquet of Saints"*, presented by Father Georges El-Khalli and Martin Ederer, intends to be an eye opener for the reader. It displays before our eyes pages of history in images and texts, shows us examples of Christian heroes - saints and martyrs, initiates us to a new way of life, and further offers us illuminating glimpse on our proper identity. Besides, from the local, it takes us to the universal, from our Community Church, it leads us to the whole Maronite Church at large.

This "bouquet" is a **guide** to the exciting works of renovation and rejuvenation of St. John Maron, our beloved Community Church in Western New York.

It is a **book of illustrations**, exhibiting before your eyes the magnificence, the majesty, the diversity and the wealth of meaning of our faith, in shapes, colors, volumes, light and vision…

It is a **teaching tool** which sketches to us and to our children the saga of our people and community, the story of our saints and the identity of our beliefs.

It is a **tribute** to our ancestors who established themselves here on this blessed land of America, one hundred years ago. Their commitment stood firm. They flourished and gave witness.

It is, last but not least, a reminder: the Church is of people, of us; the stone (here, the "Bouquet") is but the image. The Church is of those of us who live now and of those of us who lived then. - the saints, the faithful departed, as well as the living ones. Our Church here is but an image of our Church there. Our final reality is in heaven; on earth we are only the image, the image of what it is, of what will be. It is all here within the humble yet beautiful space of our worship; the "reality" is present here in the "image", all seen and touched and admired in this condensed precious Bouquet.

When we pray, we are all there together, of heaven and of earth.

I hope that this guide, prepared with care and love by its authors, will open our eyes and heart to our true Christian reality, "sharar"(confirm) us in our faith, and help us live and pass on our precious legacy

+ Stephen Hector Doueihi

Stephen Hector Doueihi, S.T.D.
Bishop
Eparchy of Saint Maron of Brooklyn
July 25, 2003

Forward

This book is a colorful bouquet of saints flourishing in the garden of the Church as portrayed in St. John Maron Church after its recent renovation. This compendium of a few saints may serve as a little window through which one can clearly see the diversity, the depth and the universality of the Maronite Church. It is a guide to the new artwork in our church and an explanation of the artwork and the significance of its symbolism. Part I introduces the context, the purpose and the rationale behind the Icons, the artwork and the stained glass windows. Part II provides a diagram presenting the Eastern and Western branches of the Catholic Church, and a list of the particular churches which developed out of different traditions. A short section about the origin of the Catholic Church precedes the table, a beautiful tapestry woven of rich traditions that form the Catholic Church. A synopsis of the identity of the Maronite Church is also included to help the reader further understand its Antiochene spiritual roots and Lebanese cultural tradition. Part III discusses the identity of the Maronite Church in eight characteristics. Part IV gives a brief history of our parish. Part V presents an overview of the new icons and stained glass. Part VI summarizes the lives of twenty saints portrayed in stained glass windows and icons. The explanation of the artwork and the symbolism of the icons are detailed in this section. The summary also includes the icon of the Pantokrator (Christ seated on the throne) and the centerpiece, which strikingly expresses the flourishing Antiochene Cross. A color picture accompanies each vignette discussing the life of that particular saint. In short, this illustrated book is itself an icon portraying our loyalty and a statement expressing our unity with the Catholic Church. It is also an expression of our love and dedication to our Maronite spiritual and religious heritage.

PART I

Introduction

In the last few years St. John Maron church underwent a major renovation, which was completed in the year 2002. During the course of the renovation new murals were added to the sanctuary and apse. A nineteen-foot icon of Christ seated on the throne now dominates the apse and sanctuary. In the center, above the tabernacle, the flourishing Antiochene Cross, bordered by scenes from Lebanon and Western New York, is a statement of the religious and the geographic roots of the parish. Four life-size icons along with arches and columns adorn the sanctuary. Starting from left to right are: St. Maron, the Blessed Mother, St. John the Apostle and St. John Maron. As part of the renovation, new stained glass windows were also installed in the interior doors of the church. Fourteen stained glass windows portray saints revered in the Maronite as well as in the Universal Church. St. Takla and St. Stephen, first female and first male martyrs, respectively, are honored in the sanctuary doors. St. Michael the Archangel and St. Jude the Apostle occupy the right side entrance while the Massabki brothers and St. Joseph the left side. Inside the main entrance stand side by side St. Ephrem, St. Anthony of the Desert, St. Rafka, St. Sharbel, Blessed Nehmatullah Al-Hardini and St. Doumit. The adjacent doors in the vestibule hold St. Therese and St. Rita. Outside the main entrance St. George and St. Elias stand as guards at the entrance of the church, nestled in the newly constructed canopy. Three transoms in stained glass are located above the doors of the main entrance of the church. Facing the Church's entrance, from the right, the first transom portrays Qadeesha or the Holy Valley, the second holds the Papal and the Patriarchal Coats of Arms, and the third presents Our

Lady of Lebanon. The stained glass windows, the icons and the artwork have greatly contributed to the solemnity of our newly remodeled church.

This renovation is in fact a dream come true. We began with the sanctuary: its marble floor, its murals, which include the icons and the artwork, and the three-tiered arches supported by the colonnade constructed above the side altars. Next came the wall marble, the main vestibule, all three church entrances, the cry rooms and the construction of the front canopy and the stained glass windows, which are mounted on the inner doors of the church. The renovations were designed to be completed before the parish centennial in 2004. Funded by many generous families and supported by the entire parish, no debts were incurred, an achievement of which we are proud. The type of religious art adopted in the new windows is a neoclassic Maronite religious art specifically designed for our parish. The size, the design and the type of art were customized for the peculiarity and specificity of our unique tradition.

The lives of the depicted saints portray the oneness of our Catholic heritage, while their complexity, richness and diverse backgrounds express our Catholic spiritual wealth. Among the Maronite saints whose lives are discussed here the reader will find Martyrs, Hermits, Confessors, Virgins, Fathers, Patriarchs and Doctors recognized by the Catholic Church. This variety confirms that the Maronite Church shares in the prophetic message and attests to its contribution to the mission of the Universal Church be it spiritual, theological, ecclesiastical, liturgical, or dogmatic. It simply shows that the Maronite Church is a beautiful enhancement adding a unique beauty to the mosaic of the larger Icon, which is the Catholic Church.

Purpose. This guide is designed to serve several purposes. It will explain to our own parish family the religious symbolism hidden in the crevices of the various icons and the artwork. It will help to educate the inquisitive minds of our youth and imbue them with a deeper understanding of the lives of the saints, especially as it introduces our Maronite saints to the Western Hemisphere. Moreover, it affords our Sunday school teachers a special catechetical tool to teach our youngsters Maronite spirituality through the lives and examples of our own saints. This is one way of initiating the younger generations into our culture, nursing them with the milk of our Maronite tradition and nourishing them with the honey of our Eastern spirituality.

For our friends in Western New York, this book is intended to introduce the Maronite tradition and the parish of St. John Maron to them. It proclaims to our visitors and neighbors that we are Catholics and in union with the Church of Rome. Although we all come from different cultural, linguistic, religious, and geographical backgrounds, we are united in our Catholic Faith and loyal to the Lord Jesus Christ and His Church. Further, it is intended to show that our religious roots date back to the Lord Jesus himself. Being Eastern does not mean being schismatic or Orthodox. The Maronite Church is an Eastern Catholic Church; it is a Patriarchal Church branching from the oldest tradition where the Apostles of Jesus were called Christians for the first time, i.e., the Church of Antioch. It is equipped with a very rich spirituality that not only prides itself in pioneering monasticism, but also a vibrant spirituality that, to this day, still thrives on monasticism and asceticism. It is important to note that despite incessant waves of religious persecution throughout its entire history, the Maronite Church remained loyal to its Catholicity and to the See of Peter whether it be in the Antioch of old or in the Rome of today. Only a small sampling of the spiritual, religious and artistic wealth of the Maronite Church is reflected in this guide.

PART II

Eastern And Western Catholic Churches

The Church is the new and continuous living Pentecost. The commissioning of the twelve Apostles was not limited to one group or race, to one nation or one geographic location. Nor was it restricted to the one particular era during which Jesus lived. Jesus commissioned the Twelve saying: *"Therefore go and make disciples of all peoples, baptizing them in the name of the Father, and of the Son, and of the Holy Spirit, and I am with you always, to the end of the age."* (Mt. 28:19, 20b) The first Church nucleus saw the light in Jerusalem, and the success of the simple fishermen was overwhelming. This success stemmed from the fact that Jesus' promises were fulfilled. The greatest witness to this success is that the Church has entered its third millennium and is stronger than ever. Starting in Jerusalem, the Apostles went to all "four corners of the world." Ensuing generations of Apostles in various locales continued in the footsteps of the first generation, and the commissioning torch was handed down to our day. Although the Church suffered a great deal of hardship and persecution, it never ceased to spread and flourish in many different countries. Enriched by the variety of particular traditions, be it the type of worship or the form of discipline, the Church at large developed different linguistic, artistic and cultural traits. From East to West the rich diversity of the faithful professed the same Catholic truth but worshipped in differing ways, each according to local customs. But all these churches which developed independently make up the One Catholic Church in the **Unity of Faith,** in the **Celebration of the Seven Sacraments.** Although they have their own particular hierarchy, they are in **communion with the Pope of Rome.**

The List of Eastern and Western Churches is as follows:

Eastern Churches:	Western Churches:
Antiochene	Roman
Armenian	
Alexandrian	
Constantinopolitan (Byzantine)	

These autonomous Churches developed their own styles of worship, spirituality, liturgy, music, theology, art and other types of disciplines stemming from location, ethnicity, culture and language. Although they are self-governed, they belong to different types of hierarchical discipline. Some are Archiepiscopal, others are Metropolitan and still others are Patriarchal. For example: the Maronite Church would be categorized as Eastern, Patriarchal and Antiochene.

The Maronite Church is the only Eastern Church which never parted from the unity of the Church of Rome nor had an Eastern Orthodox counterpart. It is worth mentioning that this Church has maintained Syriac, which is a dialect of Aramaic, the language of our Lord, to this day. At a Maronite Qurbono (Mass), anywhere around the globe, one can still hear the Institution Narrative (the words of Consecration) in Syriac, which is similar to what Jesus might have spoken at the Last Supper.

The table shows the Catholic Church and the particular traditions which have developed within it. Every Catholic can trace the origin of his or her particular church to one of these Churches.

The particular Churches, both East and West, and their respective Tradition.

WEST	EAST		EAST	EAST	EAST
Rome	**Antioch**		**Armenia**	**Alexandria**	**Constantinople**
	East Syriac	West Syriac			
Roman	Chaldean	Maronite	Armenian	Coptic	Albanian
	Malabar	Syriac		Ethiopian	Belorussian
		Malankar			Bulgarian
					Georgian
					Greek
					Greek-Melkite
					Hungarian
					Italo-Albanian
					Krizevci (Croatian)
					Romanian
					Russian
					Ruthenian
					Slovak
					Ukrainian

PART III

Identity Of The Maronite Church

Formally designated the Maronite Syriac Antiochene Church, the Maronite Church is an Eastern Catholic Church classified as Patriarchal. It is an Eastern Church but it is in union with Rome—a Western Church. Although it developed as an Eastern Church, it is not Eastern Orthodox. Its roots are in the East but its eyes looked to the Catholic West. The identity of the Maronite Church is more complex than one can imagine. Because of this unique character, eight key terms: Maronite, Syriac, Antiochene, Chalcedonian, Eastern, Monastic, Patriarchal, and Missionary are defined in order to provide a comprehensive understanding of its identity. These eight characteristics which identify the Maronite Church are as follows:

1. MARONITE. The name Maronite was given to the community of faith who adopted the spirituality and followed the example of St. Maron. It is the only Church named after its patron saint, who was a fourth century priest and hermit who left the comfort of Antioch, and chose to live in the neighboring mountainside called Cyrrhus (Qurosh in modern-day Turkey), contemplating God and living a very austere life style. There, he built for himself a roofless hut exposing his body to the elements of nature, and living a life of fasting, prayer and self-denial. This example led many anchorites to follow in his footsteps. Simon the Stylite and numerous others attempted to pursue an even harsher and more austere way of life. Because of his piety and holiness, God empowered him and worked miracles through his intercessions, granting him control over evil and performing cures of body and soul. Multitudes of faithful who came to him with sicknesses and maladies were healed. Soon after his death, his followers built a monastery at the banks of the Orontes River in which they enshrined his body. The monastery was named (Beit Maroun) a term connoting both the house of Maron and the family of Maron. The Jacobites (Syrian Orthodox) and other Christians of that vicinity gave the followers of Maron the name "Maronites."

2. SYRIAC. Syriac in language and Semitic in culture, the Maronite tradition was nourished spiritually by both the Eastern and the Western Syriac traditions. The early East Syriac tradition, i.e., Edessa and Nisibis, developed before the Greek influence. Poetic verses reflecting the theme of the feast day or the various themes of the Sunday Liturgies are employed in the Hoosoyo of our Maronite Liturgy. Renowned Church Fathers like Aphrahat the Sage, James of Saroug and St. Ephrem, the deacon and the harp of the Holy Spirit enriched its liturgy and Divine Office with their prolific poetry in Memre form.

> Hoosoyo in Syriac means atonement or forgiveness. It is virtually the highlight of the Liturgy of the Word and expresses the liturgical theme of the day. It is catechetical, exegetical and liturgical in nature and has a teaching function through which the faithful are educated in the faith. It offers a scriptural interpretation along with a series of supplications petitioning God's continuous protection and forgiveness. The Hoosoyo consists of four consecutive parts: **Proemion, Sedro, Qolo and Etro.** The **Proemion** is the introductory prayer, which offers praise, worship and magnificent titles to Christ. The Sedro is the heart of the Hoosoyo and through its catechetical function it reflects God's plan of salvation and explains the theme of the particular Sunday, feast day, or saint of the day being celebrated. It further presents, in a litany form, petitions asking for the Lord's favor and assistance. **Qolo** in Syriac means hymn and is found in various liturgical celebrations. It is poetic in nature and is composed of several verses in metrical form. In the Hoosoyo, however, the Qolo is a response to the series of supplications and petitions whereby it magnifies the theme of the Hoosoyo and accentuates its character. **Etro** in Syriac means sweet perfume (of incense) and is the conclusion of the

Hoosoyo. It summarizes the petitions of the Church who asks God to accept its precious offering which is consumed and raised to the heights. The burning of incense is par excellence an act of purification; it further connotes symbolism of our good deeds that are acceptable to God.

Memre (singular Memro) is a form of poetry that was introduced by the early Fathers of the Syriac Church. The verses are rhythmic and have the same number of syllables, and the terminal sounds of lines or of words correspond. It is in essence a metrical form and is found in many Maronite liturgical prayers, especially in some parts of the Hoosoyo.

The Western Syriac tradition, i.e., Antioch, was exemplified by Church orators, theologians and historians like John Chrysostom (before his appointment to Constantinople), bishop Theodoret, and Theodore of Mopsuestia. Located in Asia Minor, this Syriac-speaking territory stretched eastward from the Mediterranean Sea in Southern Turkey through Northern Syria and Northern Iraq, following the ancient caravan trails that crossed into India (see map below). This religiously fertile ground between Antioch, Edessa and Nisibis cultivated the Syriac language, which was an Aramaic dialect spoken by Our Lord. Syriac, to the present day, is still the official liturgical language of the Maronite Church. Poetic imagery, typology (a form of Biblical interpretation), liturgical mysticism and spiritual symbolism originated in the Syriac Church and influenced the Maronite Tradition to this day.

3. ANTIOCHENE. The Maronite Church is categorized as Antiochene because it branched out of the Church of Antioch. It was the See of St. Peter about a decade before he extended his mission to Rome and the rest of the Roman Empire. According to Acts 11:26 "It was in Antioch that the Apostles were called Christians for the first time." Antioch (Antakya, in modern-day Turkey) is the oldest hierarchical Catholic Church established among the five greatest traditions of the Church, followed by Jerusalem, Alexandria, Rome and Constantinople (see map below). Geographically, Antioch was strategically located, linking the Roman Empire to its eastern provinces. Thus it became a center where

communication, commerce, learning, culture and arts were extensively cultivated. The Antiochene School of thought pioneered typology, a biblical interpretation which drew a parallel between people and events in the Old Testament and people and events in the New Testament, centering them all around the life and the ministry of Christ. The spiritual, theological and ecclesiastical heritage of Antioch gave us many famous names such as St. Ignatius, the second Patriarch after St. Peter, who organized the hierarchical order of the Church: the ministries known today as deacon, priest and bishop. Furthermore, it was Ignatius who before anyone else applied the term "Catholic" to the Universal Church. More great names who added to the fame of the Antiochene tradition are Libanios the famous orator; Lucian the biblical scholar; Theodore of Mopsuestia, the great theologian; Theodoret of Cyrrhus, the renowned historian and bishop; and St. Theophilus, to mention just a few.

4. CHALCEDONIAN. The Maronites adopted and taught the dogma of the Council of Chalcedon, fought for it and defended it with their lives for many centuries. This important Ecumenical Church Council was held in 451 A.D. in the city of Chalcedon located east of Constantinople across the water, and on the southern banks of the Black Sea (see map below). This Church Council condemned the heresy of the Monophysites, which held that in Christ there was only one nature. The Catholic Church confirmed the teaching of the Council of Chalcedon that in Christ there are two natures, human and divine. The Church excommunicated Eutyches and all his followers who opposed the Chalcedonian dogma. The Maronite Church is categorized as Chalcedonian so that it is differentiated from two heresies, which resulted in the creation of the Monophysite and the Nestorian churches of the time.

5. EASTERN. In culture, geography, language and spirituality, the Maronite Church belongs to the family of the Eastern Churches. It developed out of the Church of Antioch, which is situated in the East. Having its Semitic culture rooted in the East, characterized by the Syriac language and adorned by its distinct liturgy and monastic spirituality, the Maronite Church developed a unique character of its own. It is an Eastern Church but it is in union with Rome—a Western

Church. It was born in the East but it follows the Gregorian calendar rather than the Julian or lunar calendar. It is an Eastern Church but not Eastern Orthodox. It is Antiochene but neither Monophysite nor Monothelite. It is however, Chalcedonian, Patriarchal and deeply rooted in Monasticism. Further, it is one of the twenty-two "sui iuris" or autonomous Eastern Churches. Although completely independent, it professes the same Catholic faith and is in full union with the Church of Rome. In fact, the Maronite Church prides itself as the only Eastern Church whose communion with the Church of Rome, throughout its entire history, was never interrupted.

6. MONASTIC. The Maronite Church first saw the light from the shining sun of a prominent monastery. St. Maron, its founder, was a monk and a hermit who devised a unique method of monasticism. St. John Maron, its first Patriarch, was a monk and a graduate of the Monastery of St. Maron. This monastery became a center of learning and attracted students and scholars, laity and clergy, who were trained and educated in various fields and skills, not just in academics and humanities. Becoming more than just a school, this monastery later developed a community of faith around it who professed and lived faithfully the ascetic and monastic tradition of St. Maron. Thus, this monastery was called Beit Maroun, which connotes the house as well as the family of Maron. It was from this monastery that the Maronite Church was born. The monastic spirituality in all of its forms is quite evident in the Liturgy and in the Divine Office. The monasticism of St. Anthony the Great and St. Pachomius of Egypt along with the Syriac asceticism of St. Maron and St. Simon the Stylite of Antioch have shaped and influenced the monastic spirituality of Beit Maroun. Inheriting such a rich monastic tradition, Maronite saintly patriarchs, bishops, monks and religious, from the dawn of monasticism through the Middle Ages linked the same monasticism of St. Anthony and St. Maron to that of St. Sharbel, St. Rafka and Blessed Nehmatullah Al-Hardini of our day.

7. PATRIARCHAL. The Maronite Church is Patriarchal in hierarchy, which makes it quite different from being Metropolitan or Archiepiscopal. It is a self-governed church "sui iuris" with its own particular law, liturgy, music, spirituality and theology developing out of its own geographic location and characterized by its cultural and linguistic traits. It is a community of faith, a Church in the full sense of the word, guided by bishops and headed by the Patriarch, which can trace its foundation to one or more of the Twelve Apostles of Jesus. The Maronite Church is a Patriarchal Church where the Patriarch is the leader, the father and the symbol of its unity.

8. MISSIONARY. From its inception, the Maronite Church has been a pilgrim church both literally and figuratively. Originating in the East, it is now spread all around the globe. Starting out of the Monastery of St. Maron at the dawn of the fifth century, it spread to the various parts of the Middle East but mostly it spread southward to Mount Lebanon where it took root, was confirmed and became well established. The Maronites shaped Lebanon as a political entity and made of it a national homeland for the last 1400 years. Due to religious persecution and political instability in the region since the middle of the nineteenth century, the Maronite Church experienced an extensive migration to the Western Hemisphere, where Eparchial jurisdictions have already taken shape. An Apostolic Visitator in Europe, an Eparchy in each of the following countries: Argentina, Australia, Brazil, Canada, Mexico and two in the United States of America attest to the immigrant character of the Maronite Church.

Patriarch Estefan Al-Duwayhi (1670-1704) defines the Maronite Church according to three principles: (a) loyalty to Maron, (b) loyalty to the Roman Church and (c) loyalty to Mount Lebanon. The following definition is translated from the original Arabic of the text of the Maronite Patriarchal Council.

Loyalty to Maron was based on history, vivid memory and tradition, which remained intact through centuries because it adopted the Antiochene spirituality, monasticism and Chalcedonian theology. According to his most recent letter regarding the Maronite Patriarchal Council, Patriarch Sfeir claims: this loyalty links the Maronites to the person of the Patriarch who is "the leader of their church, the protector and the symbol of their unity."

Loyalty to the Roman Church and to the successor of Peter became the continuation of the loyalty to Maron. History witnessed the uninterrupted loyalty of the followers of Maron to the Roman Church existing between the Maronite Church and the Church of Rome and between the successor of John Maron and the successor of Peter, all in spite of difficulties and tribulations. This loyalty is expressed within the framework of the unity of the body of Christ through many members.

Loyalty to Mount Lebanon stems from the fact that once the nation of Maron was established in Lebanon, it resulted in the establishment of the Patriarchate there. Mount Lebanon and thereafter Lebanon is the greatest achievement the Maronites accomplished during 1400 years, whereby they created a political entity which afforded them a chance to come out of isolation and a place where freedom could be realized in all of its meanings. This achievement by the Maronites solidified the Maronite nation in Mount Lebanon and confirmed the Partriarchate as a gathering and a unifying agent during severe political and religious difficulties.

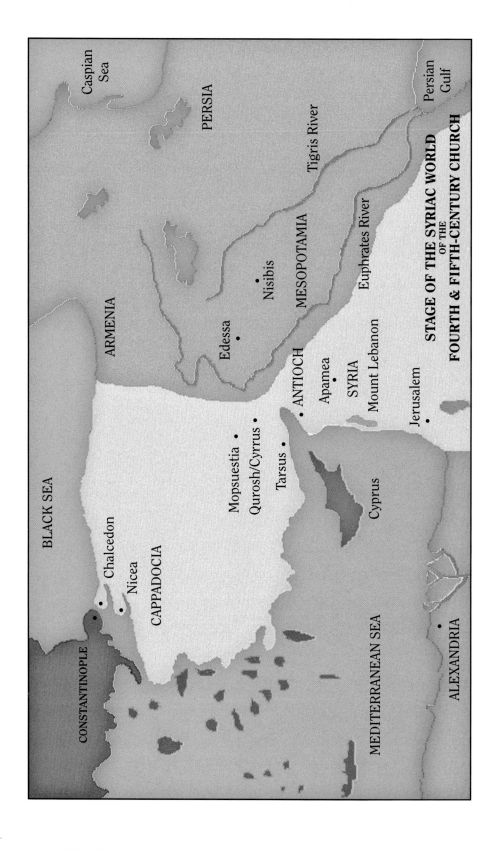

STAGE OF THE SYRIAC WORLD
OF THE
FOURTH & FIFTH-CENTURY CHURCH

PART IV

A Brief History Of Our Parish

Bishop Charles Colton originally set up St. John Maron Church in Buffalo in March of 1904 to serve the Maronite Lebanese (or "Syrians" a term used to refer globally to both those from Lebanon and Syria). Hard times in Lebanon under the Turkish heel resulting from a combination of discrimination, persecution and starvation— sometimes all three of those together—led many to emigrate to other parts of the world, including the United States. Many Lebanese had been attracted to the Buffalo area for the business potential of the 1901 Pan-American Exposition. Rev. Anthony Zoghby laid the groundwork for the parish in 1903, and Rev. George Aziz established a church for his people. The cornerstone of the original church and rectory, a converted store and house located at 454 Seneca St. between Louisiana and Spring streets, was installed in March 1904. The church was dedicated on June 26 of that same year.

St. John Maron quickly established missions to other Lebanese enclaves in Western New York, forming Our Lady of Lebanon in Niagara Falls, New York, which became an autonomous parish in 1914, and St. Joseph in Olean, New York, which became autonomous in 1919.

The parish began building a new church in 1919, this time located at South Division and Cedar Streets. This building was a practical combination church/school with the church on the first floor, and the school on the second floor. It was designed by an architect known only as Mr. Hill. Ground was broken in October 1919, and the new church was dedicated on November 1, 1920.

In 1952, Rev. Monsignor Francis Shemalie requested permission from Bishop Joseph Burke to build a new church, citing the fact that only 15% of the parish still actually lived around Cedar Street, and that the parishioners wanted a more elaborate building of which they could be proud. No immediate decision appears to have been made, but when the Ellicott District Redevelopment Project was unveiled, both St. John Maron and nearby St. Lucy were staring at a bulldozer blade. Consequently, Rev. Peter Sfeir, pastor at the time, laid the cornerstone of the present church in 1961. Generous parishioners had donated twelve acres of land for the new church on Wehrle Drive in Williamsville the previous year. Originally two statues, one of Saint John Maron, the other of Saint Maron, topped the towers of the church. The statues were later replaced with the existing twin Antiochene (Maronite) crosses.

As a result of Vatican II reforms encouraging the Catholic Eastern Churches to recover, maintain and perpetuate their unique heritage, and the growth in number of Maronites in the United States it became feasible for a Maronite Eparchy (diocese) to be established. As a result, St. John Maron, once a parish under the jurisdiction of the Diocese of Buffalo, is now under the jurisdiction of the Eparchy of St. Maron of Brooklyn. The parish grew precipitously during the civil war that ravaged Lebanon through most of the 1970s and the 1980s, as many thousands of Maronite Lebanese refugees fled their homeland. As the parish grew, so did its physical plant: the parish center was built in 1962; the rectory in 1967; the shrine of St. Sharbel Makhlouf in 1978 (redesigned in 2002); and the Maronite Education Center in 1985. The Church underwent a major repair, renovation and beautification project between 2001 and 2002.

St. John Maron parish has been blessed throughout its history with talented and devoted priests, both its pastors and its assistant priests. St. John Maron's pastors, who guided the parish through its growth, its changes, and its crises merit recognition:

Rev. Antoun A Zoghby
(1903-1904)

Rev. George Aziz
(1904-1908)

Rev. Msgr. Francis Shemalie
(1908-1959)

Rev. Peter Sfeir
(1959-1968)

Rev. Maroun Abi Nader
(1968-1969)

Rev. Msgr. Joseph D. Joseph
(1969-1996)

Rev. Georges Y. El-Khalli
(1996-present)

PART V

Overview Of The New Artwork

In the apse reigns Christ the *Pantokrator* attended by two beautiful *peacocks*. The Syriac and English inscription on the book he holds reads: "I am the Way the Truth and the Life." Christ the Pantokrator is always depicted in Eastern iconography and spirituality seated on a throne and accompanied by the Blessed Mother and John, the Beloved Disciple, who later became the great Evangelist. The Blessed Mother is always standing on Jesus' right and St. John on his left.

Just underneath the throne of Christ, the **Antiochene Cross** dominates the centerpiece. It presents a particular statement about the Maronites in Western New York, who came from Lebanon to the Niagara Frontier, and explains their heritage in two scenes, to the left and to the right of the Cross. On the left is a typical Lebanese village, a monastery and a mountain covered with snow, and on the right is Niagara Falls and the Basilica of Our Lady of Victory. The Antiochene Cross is painted to simulate the texture of the Cedars of Lebanon and it is rooted in both East and West, two vital sources of the Maronite Tradition. It expresses oneness of the Maronites, linking us to our ancestors, and shows our unity with the Catholic Church. The sprouting leaves on the wooden cross symbolize the vibrant community, the vigorous youth and the continuous presence of the Maronite Church from its inception until the present day and particularly in Western New York.

Bordering the two lower sides of Christ, the icon of the **Blessed Mother** is placed on its right and that of **St. John the Evangelist** on its left. On the far left above the side-altar, **St. Maron** stands in front of the monastery of *Beit Maroun* blessing his flock. On the far right, a smiling **St. John Maron**, the first Maronite Patriarch, stands firm in the middle of the storm of heresies and persecutions. The icons of St.

Maron and St. John Maron are crowned with three-tiered arches and supported by two sets of colonnades. Three-dimensional arches and columns are painted throughout the sanctuary to frame its doors and icons, while the arch of the apse is ornamented with jewels and pictured as the crown of our Lord.

The impressive apse dominating the sanctuary forms a semi-circular middle-eastern-shaped arch. Two columns were painted to look like they support the arch of the apse. The apse and its arch are typical of Maronite church architecture and house the *Pantokrator*—the most dominant icon in our church. Taking the concept of arches and columns as a starting point, the whole remodeling idea revolved around this theme. Three-tiered arches above the side altars, supported by three sets of columns to hold the tiers, were designed to correspond to the semi-circular center arch and to create a symmetrical balance in the sanctuary. For the sake of artistic continuity and consistency, the icons and doors of the sanctuary, the stained glass windows set in the wooden doors inside the church, and those enshrined in the outside canopy also adopt the same theme of arches and columns. Even the tablets forming the book in the hand of Christ are shaped like the new icons that are found throughout our remodeled church. The newly built three-tiered arches and all the icons are painted with beautiful bright colors. The supporting beams of the ceiling, the colonnade, the pews, the doors and the wood trim are all painted with a bright reddish cherry finish to match the Rojo Alicante marble color, which is the color of the columns of the altars. The stained glass windows are custom made for our church doors, and the neoclassic Maronite religious style in which the various saints are designed is inspired by ancient Syriac art and typical of our Maronite Tradition. This addition of artwork, iconography and stained glass windows, along with the new color of pews, doors and wood trim, give our church a more majestic, richer look that conveys the Maronite spiritual identity and heritage.

Fourteen stained glass windows are set in the inner doors of the Church in the shape of the middle-eastern arch and portray Maronite saints as well as saints from the Universal Church. The sanctuary doors honor the first female and the first male martyrs, St. Takla and St. Stephen, situated on the outer sides of the icons of the Blessed Mother and St. John the Evangelist, respectively. By the side of powerful-looking St. John Maron stand mighty St. Michael and St. Jude overseeing the right foyer, while the Blessed Massabki brothers and St. Joseph adorn the left foyer. St. Doumit, Blessed Nehmatullah Al-Hardini, St. Sharbel, St. Rafka, St. Anthony of the Desert and St. Ephrem stand side by side as hosts at the entrance to welcome you to the church. Watching over the vestibule are a mother and a nun, St. Rita and St. Theresa respectively, symbols of spiritual strength and patrons of mothers and children. They provide affection and protection to the adjacent cry rooms. St. George and St. Elias stand vigilantly guarding the church's main entrance and are nestled in two gothic-arch windows in the newly constructed outside canopy. The gothic-shaped arches are designed to match the outer windows of the Church.

Three Transoms in stained glass are located over the doors of the Church's main entrance. The center transom holds the Papal and the Patriarchal Coats of Arms and testifies to the nature and Catholicity of our parish. The two border transoms, Our Lady of Lebanon and Qadeesha or the Holy Valley, depict scenery and holy sites from Lebanon.

The Papal and the Patriarchal Coats of Arms. The center transom exhibits the Papal Coat of Arms on the left and the Patriarchal Coat of Arms on the right. St. Peter's Square and the Basilica symbolize the Vatican and the Roman Patriarchate (the papacy). Bkerke, the Patriarchal residence in Lebanon, is chosen as the symbol of the Antiochene Patriarchate. They portray the Eastern and the Western Sees of St. Peter. They stand side by side expressing the everlasting unity which exists between the Maronite Church and the Church of

Rome. The mountain, the sea and the ship shown between the two Holy Sees emphasize the closeness and the unity, rather than the distance and the separation between them. Because of centuries of persecution the only means of travel for the Maronites was the boat, the Phoenician ship, which we inherited from our ancestors. Ocean, ship, mountain, cedars and blue skies: all these translate into the earthly paradise of the Maronites.

Qadeesha or the Holy Valley. Located on the left side as you exit the church, this transom expresses the rich spirituality and the simplicity of the monastery of Our Lady of Qannoubeen which is located in the heart of the Holy Valley. It further illustrates the Coronation of the Blessed Mother—the fresco that exists in the apse of this monastery. Mary, the Queen of the Universe, is enthroned in Heaven and worshipped by the Seraphim and the Cherubim. God the Father, creator of the Universe, crowns the Queen with His right hand while He holds the globe with His left. Christ, seated on the right hand of God the Father, shares in the crowning of the Queen as He holds the Cross, the symbol of victory over death, in His right hand. The Holy Spirit hovers over the Queen's head and participates in the crowning. To the right of the coronation scene is the monastery of Our Lady of Qannoubeen, which for centuries served as the Patriarchal residence. Hewn in a huge rock, this cave is itself the monastery. Only the façade of this cave can be seen. Our holy patriarchs lived and governed the Maronite Church out of this cave. To the left is an awe-inspiring view of Qadeesha, which is somber, quiet, and solemn. From the dawn of the Maronite ages to the computer age, Qadeesha was never abandoned; saintly patriarchs, bishops, hermits and monks were its constant

companions. The monasteries and hermitages of Qadeesha are still in full operation to our day.

Our Lady of Lebanon. Located on the right side as you exit the church, this transom shows Our Lady of Lebanon on the hill of Harissa overlooking the Bay of Jounieh—one of the prettiest sights in the Middle East. Our Lady of Lebanon, in dazzling white, dominates the scene. The tower of the newly constructed Basilica stands next to it as a powerful symbol blending antiquity and modernity. The celestial blue, the color of the Blessed Mother, paints the horizons and connects sea and sky denoting the everlasting purity and the infinite clarity of the Lady who, for centuries, has protected Lebanon and the Maronites. Also included in this beautiful scenery is a view of the city of Jounieh and a chain of mountains with the holy and everlasting Cedars of Lebanon. In the Maronite litany dedicated to the Blessed Mother, Mary is called upon as the Cedar of Lebanon and the Cedar of our Faith.

The Lives Of The Saints

(A) THE MURALS

The *Pantokrator* (Christ Enthroned)

Dominating the apse of the sanctuary is a large likeness of Christ enthroned as ruler and teacher (the *Pantokrator,* a depiction of Jesus as creator of the universe common in the early Christian Semitic and Byzantine East). His face is modeled after the image on the shroud of Turin as revealed in the famous 1898 photographic negative. His features are Semitic, a more realistic depiction than the common Euro-American portrayal of Jesus as a man with light complexion, straight light brown hair and bluish eyes. The composition of the enthroned *Pantokrator* within an arch is inspired by an illustration found in the sixth-century *Rabbula Gospel.* This Syriac manuscript is an ancient illustrated Maronite text assembled by *Rabbula,* an early Maronite monk and artist. The colors employed in the *Pantokrator* mural are significant. The white alb of Jesus signifies His priesthood and purity and the mantle signifies His Crucifixion. The royal purple cloak represents both His passion and death and also His dominion over all creation. The golden sash represents Jesus' resurrection in glory. Jesus' throne and footstool represent His dominion over both Heaven and earth. The footstool is depicted as granite and pearl and the throne is depicted as marble. The marble and pearl, exquisite and rare materials, signify earthly royalty and the kingship of Christ. The green seat cushions and trim represent nature. The brown foot cushion represents the color of dirt, symbolizing earth as his footstool. Jesus holds two tablets as an open book—shaped in the same way as the arches over the

I Am
The Way
And The Truth
And The Life

John 14:6

A Colorful Bouquet of Saints

murals in the sanctuary and over the side altars—on which is written in both Syriac and English, *"I am the Way, the Truth and the Life." (John 14:6)*. Jesus' right hand is giving the ancient Antiochene Eastern blessing, which shows his role and destiny from the Father and the Trinity to bring humanity life and to restore humanity's broken relationship with the Father as the result of sin.

The Peacocks

Two Peacocks frame the *Pantokrator* in the apse, ancient Maronite symbols of the Resurrection also found in the *Rabbula Gospel*. Actually the peacock imagery predates Christianity, having first served as a pagan symbol for the goddess Juno and also for renewal and immortality. In the early Christian era, the peacock became the symbol of immortality and resurrection and appeared regularly in depiction of Mary, the Apostles, Evangelists and the Pentecost.

The Antiochene Cross (Central Mural)

Beneath Jesus the teacher in the lower center arch is a representation of the heritage of the people of Saint John Maron parish. Dominating the scene is a large Maronite Antiochene Cross, here depicted as a living tree bearing the dark texture of the Cedar of Lebanon, the national symbol of Lebanon. The sprouting leaves underscore the fact that this tree is alive. It grows out of the Eucharist, which is in the tabernacle under the tree's trunk. The Antiochene Cross is basically a Patriarchal cross. It symbolizes the Unity and the Trinity of God, the vertical post signifying one God, and the crossbeams representing Father, Son and Holy Spirit. Its design was inspired by the many early Trinitarian and Christological heresies that stiffened the Maronites' loyalty to authentic Catholic Apostolic teaching. Geographic and religious roots inspired the design of the murals on either side of the cross.

To the left of the Antiochene Cross are represented the Lebanese origins of the parish. Depicted is a mountain village, typical of Lebanese topography, whereas the religious roots are symbolized by the Monastery of Saint Anthony the Great, known as Mar Antonios Koz-hayah, whose prominence lasted for many centuries in Lebanon. It represents the strong monastic influence on Maronite Christianity and its spirituality. The snow-white mountains represent the origins of the name Lebanon—*Laban*, or "white"—because the mountains of Lebanon are snow-capped throughout the year.

To the right of the cross is an image of the American roots of the parish. Western New York is represented by Niagara Falls, which is its most outstanding topographical feature. Our Lady of Victory Basilica in Lackawanna, the most visible symbol of Catholicity in the region, reflects our religious roots in Western New York. From Lebanon to Western New York, from then until now, the Maronite Church and the Antiochene Cross and its traditions are vibrant and flourishing.

To either side of the lower center arch are two smaller arches representing the two followers of Jesus who remained with him when he was crucified, his Mother and John the Beloved Disciple.

The Blessed Mother

To the left of the cross, and looking up to Jesus the teacher is His mother, Mary, with her hands positioned to portray her as the mediatrix, or intermediary of graces between Jesus enthroned in Heaven and his people struggling in this world. For Catholics, Mary is worthy of special veneration as the Mother of God. She was conceived without sin, and she remained a virgin after conceiving and bearing Jesus through the power of the Holy Spirit. Eastern Christians developed an especially fervent devotion to Mary, whom they venerated with eloquent prayers and poetry. It was also in the East where so many heresies arose about her status and role with respect to the nature of Jesus as God and as man. The Maronites have traditionally maintained a strong devotion to Mary, a tradition strengthened by the poetry and writings of Saint Ephrem. Some of the most beautiful prayers and devotions in the Maronite tradition honor Mary, the Mother of God. Litanies of the Blessed Virgin Mary encompass her entire life from her mother's womb until her Dormition, and include the Mystery of Salvation.

Although she was grief-stricken during the Crucifixion of her Son, Mary is here presented with a slight smile and shown in a quiet perfection, amidst blooming spring flowers. She is depicted in an eternal spring and possesses youth and beauty, which every human wishes to possess forever.

Saint John the Evangelist

To the right of the cross is Saint John the Beloved Disciple, the Apostle and Evangelist, looking up to the cross and to Jesus in Heaven for his inspiration to write his Gospel, his letters and the Book of Revelation. He is writing in Syriac the opening verses of his Gospel: *"In the beginning was the Word, and the Word was with God, and the Word was God. He was in the beginning with God" (John 1:1-2)*. John was the son of Zebedee the fisherman and Mary of Salome, and is described in the Gospels as the one Jesus loved. He was the Savior's closest friend and confidant. When Jesus was crucified, John was the only Apostle to stay with Jesus and His mother Mary, while the others were in hiding. John was the greatest witness to Jesus' life, sayings and miracles, and often provides us details and insights not found in the synoptic Gospel

accounts. He completes and corroborates those accounts, and addresses early heresies. As Jesus was dying on the Cross, He entrusted John with caring for Mary, which he did until her Dormition in Jerusalem. According to Tradition, John led that funeral service. After Paul's execution in Rome, we find John in Ephesus (modern-day Turkey), and Tertullian and Irenaeus recount that he was in Rome, where the emperor Domition ordered him to be boiled in oil. Although he shared in the ordeal of martyrdom, he miraculously came out of the boiling oil unharmed. He was exiled to the Greek island of Patmos, where he wrote one of the most difficult books of the Bible, the Book of Revelation, which added to his already impressive output of his Gospel and three other letters. John, the youngest of the Apostles, died a very old man. In many respects, John the Evangelist is the model Christian. He is portrayed in the Gospels with his head on Jesus' chest, a reflection of his profound love for the Savior and also his insistence on keeping his head close to Jesus' heart, his total submission to the authentic teachings of Jesus. He loved Jesus freely, generously and completely, and even fear of the authorities could not keep him away from Jesus on the Cross. Saint John the Evangelist's feast is May 8.

The background of the St. John Icon, unlike the florid background of the Icon of the Blessed Virgin Mary, shows the arid desolation of the desert. The desolation represents the fact that John was exiled for a time, and also his abandonment of all distractions so that he could concentrate solely on the words of Jesus which were abundantly revealed to him.

Saint Maron (died 407): Left Side Altar Mural
Saint Maron is the father of the Maronite Catholic Church. Most of what we know about him comes from an account by Theodoret, the bishop of Qurosh, who lived from 393-457. According to Theordoret, Saint Maron spent most of his life as a hermit monk who nonetheless also became famous for his charity among the people. He decided to live as a hermit not far from Antioch, the city where the followers of Jesus were called Christians for the first time (Acts 11:26). Maron retreated to a rugged mountain area, establishing a hermitage between Qurosh and Aleppo, living out in the open air. The exact location identified by Patriarch Stephen Al-Duwayhi's research in the

أَبَانَا
مَارُون

eighteenth century—and supported by archeology—is Mt. Al-Yambos near the village of Kefar-Nabo. According to Theodoret and many other later historians, Saint Maron pioneered a new monastic asceticism establishing the following principles: solitude, living exposed to the elements with minimal shelter, and continuous union with God. Although he had lived an austere life in Antioch, Saint Maron felt he needed to still do more, and that need led him to seek a life of more prayer, mortification and self-denial. After Maron embraced this type of spirituality, he influenced many disciples to follow in his footsteps. Saint Simon the Stylite, well-known both in the East and in the West, tried to outdo his master by living year-round on top of a pillar, without the benefit of any shelter. Saint Maron converted a pagan temple into a church, and many of the local people flocked to him for spiritual guidance and cures. Soon all the area of Antioch learned of his spiritual zeal and sound dogma. The well-known Patriarch of Antioch, Saint John Chrysostom, writing from his exile in 404-405, expressed his admiration for Maron: "Be sure that we never cease to remember you wherever we are, because of the high place you have in our esteem." Saint Maron died in 407, was acclaimed spiritual master, and a church was built over his tomb. Soon after Maron's death, his followers built a monastery in the Apamea region at Qala'at-Al-Modeeq near the Orontes River. This great Monastery of Saint Maron—called Beit Maroun, or the "House of Maron"—became the spiritual center, loyal to the Catholic Church and to the decrees of the Council of Chalcedon.

Saint Maron is depicted as the father of a new nation blessing his people. Left of him is the pagan temple he converted into a Christian church and right of him is the Orontes River and the monastery that developed from his ascetic tradition, *Beit Maroun*. The desolate mountains behind him represent the mountains of Qurosh (Cyrrhus), which he made famous. Saint Maron's feast is February 9.

Saint John Maron (died 707): Right Side Altar Mural
Saint John Maron was the first patriarch of the Maronites. He was born in Sarum, near Antioch, possibly in the 630's. Originally named John, he descended from Frankish nobility and Middle Eastern backgrounds. He excelled in his studies, first at the Monastery of Saint Maron—from

Saint
John
Maron

which he took the additional name Maron—and then in Constantinople. As a priest, he became a versatile scholar and a prolific writer on pedagogy, rhetoric, the sacraments, church law and liturgy. He composed a special Anaphora (Eucharistic Prayer) for the Maronite liturgy, "The Anaphora of Saint John Maron, patriarch of Antioch," still in use today, which is used especially for the sick and the oppressed. He also defended authentic Catholic teachings—upholding the decrees of the Council of Chalcedon (451) against the Monophysites, heretics who held that Jesus had only one nature, and the Monothelites, who argued that Jesus had only one will. In the process, he strengthened the loyal Christians surrounded by heretics, Muslims or other non-Christians, and even won many of the heretics to the Catholic faith. He also became famous for his love of the poor, the sick and the suffering, and especially for the many miracles he worked curing the sick and dying among his flock.

Saint John Maron's talents did not go unnoticed. The Holy See consecrated John Maron bishop of Batroun, a Lebanese coastal town located between Byblos and Tripoli, to keep the Maronites unified with Rome, to challenge the Monophysites and to defend Christendom against the Arabs. By this time, John Maron had also become an important political leader who commanded a powerful army, the Maradites. This Maronite army held the Islamic Ummayyad Arab threat at bay, and also assisted the Byzantine Empire in holding back similar Arab advances during the great era of Arab expansion. So powerful were the Maradites that the Byzantines referred to them as "The Brass Wall" of the Byzantine Empire. At the peak of their influence and power, Maradite territory extended from Palestine to Armenia. Meanwhile, constant persecutions and political and military struggle in Syria left the patriarchal see of Antioch vacant in the later seventh century. During that time, several Antiochene patriarchs resided in Constantinople, the splendid capital of the Byzantine Empire, while holding the title "Patriarch of Antioch." The Maronite Christians left behind, however, felt abandoned, and elected John Maron the Patriarch of Antioch in 685. Pope Sergius I enthusiastically approved his election as "Patriarch of Antioch and All the East." These developments alarmed the Byzantines, who had grown proud of the fact that Constantinople had become a dual patriarchal seat. Consequently, they began to resent the power and the independence of the Maronites, and they tried to seize Saint John Maron. One-time allies became enemies, and the Maradites now had to defend Maronite religious traditions and political independence against powerful Byzantine armies that pursued John Maron and the Maradites, who retreated to the mountains of Lebanon. After a pitched battle, the Maradites defeated Byzantine forces on both fronts, Smar-Jbeil and Amyoun. With the Maradites, Saint John Maron brought peace to the mountain, and began building churches and monasteries throughout the region. He established his patriarchal see at Kefar-Hay in the mountains above Batroun, where he built a monastery. It is believed that he brought the skull of Saint Maron, *Reesh Moran* (meaning "the head of our Lord,") with him from Antioch, and the monastery came to bear that name. Although Saint John Maron ultimately had to retreat with the Maronites to the mountains, he did, however, successfully defend the Maronite identity from heretics, the Arabs, and the Byzantine Empire. John Maron not only constructed a monastery, but also the hierarchical structure and identity of the Maronite Church. As a result, when the Byzantine Empire severed its religious ties with the papacy in 1054, the Maronites remained Catholic. The Maronites are the only Eastern Catholic Church without a non-Catholic equivalent. Saint John Maron died in Kefar-Hay in 707.

Saint John Maron is portrayed standing firm in the middle of a storm, not a windstorm, but a storm of heresy, oppression and persecution swirling his vestments about him as he destroys heretical writings with his crosier and crushes the snake of evil under his foot. In the background stands the great monastery on the mountainside of Kefar-Hay, which is still standing today as a testimony to the great legacy of the continuous presence of the Maronites in the region. Saint John Maron's feast is March 2.

The Lives Of The Saints

(B) THE STAINED GLASS WINDOWS

This guide to the saints portrayed in the stained glass windows starts with the main entrance and proceeds to the sanctuary of the church.

Saint George (died 303)

Saint George is normally portrayed slaying a dragon, and that portrayal is based on the most famous story about him. According to that story, Saint George came to the city of Sylene in Libya. In a nearby swamp lived a dragon which the people wished to kill, but its breath made it too awful to approach, so they prevented it from coming any closer to the city by feeding it two sheep per day. When the sheep supply ran out, humans were substituted. When the lot had fallen to the king's daughter to be the next victim, nobody wished to take her place, and she went out to meet her doom. Saint George intervened and attacked the dragon. He bound the dragon by the neck, and the king's daughter herself led the dragon into the city, where people began to flee in terror. There, Saint George told them to take courage. If they would be baptized Christians, he would slay the dragon. The whole city converted, and Saint George slew the beast. The whole story may well have a more figurative sense, the dragon being evil slain through conversion and baptism. Saint George was martyred in 303, probably in Lydda, Palestine, during the persecutions of the Roman emperor Diocletian.

There are many variations to the basic dragon story—especially with respect to its location. For the Lebanese, the dragon episode took place

in Beirut. But it is a fact that Saint George actually lived. The variations simply attest that Saint George was so highly venerated everywhere—from Byzantium to Lebanon to North Africa to western Europe—that all wanted to claim him as their own. Devotion to Saint George, a soldier from Cappodocia, may date to the 4th century, and it is possible that the Emperor Constantine himself built the first church in his honor in Constantinople. The Lebanese developed a strong devotion to Saint George, for whom they named the bay immediately north of Beirut, its shores the home of early Christian settlements, and Beirut itself was the first Christian city to dedicate a cathedral to Saint George. After his death he came to be frequently confused with Adonis among both Christians and non-Christians throughout the Middle East, and also with the prophet Elias under the name *El Khader,* or "The Green Verdant Pasture." By the 1300s Saint George also came to be recognized as the patron and protector of England.

The window of Saint George—a protector saint— is placed in the porch outside the church to guard the entrance. The Saint George window shows him slaying the dragon with a spear. The flame-like flag on the upper end of the spear signifies his martyrdom, and his round shield signifies the wheel of spikes to which he was affixed before he was roasted over a fire until dead. His feast is April 23.

Saint Elias (c. 935 B.C.)

The Old Testament prophet Elias or Elijah the Tishbite is introduced in the First Book of Kings, predicting a great drought and famine as the result of the Kingdom of Israel's breaking faith with their God. Many of the Israelites—including King Ahab—had begun to worship Baal, god of the Phoenicians, the precursors of the Lebanese. During the drought, Elias requested food and water of a Canaanite widow and her son, who were facing certain starvation. She faithfully tended to his needs—against her better judgment—but as a result, her meager supplies of flour, water and oil lasted a whole year. When her only son died, Elias brought him back to life for the woman, showing he was a man of God. Elias also challenged the Hebrew followers of Baal to a contest to show them the true God. Their god did not respond when they made sacrifices to him. Then Elias prepared his sacrifice to the God of Israel, dousing it with water in order to make it even more difficult for the fires of heaven to consume it. When fire came down

from heaven, it nonetheless consumed everything. The people turned against Baal, reestablished their loyalty to the true God, and the clouds opened up, ending the drought. All these events took place in Zaraphat, now Sarafand, a Lebanese coastal town located between Beirut and Sidon. Meanwhile, Elias hunted down the prophets of Baal and killed them, but ultimately he had to flee the remaining followers of Baal, which included King Ahab of Israel, who wanted to kill him. Eventually he got King Ahab to repent, but he faced similar challenges with Ahab's successors. Elias hid from his persecutors by crossing the Jordan River into present-day Jordan. From there the Second Book of Kings recounts that "a flaming chariot and flaming horses came...and Elias went up to heaven in a whirlwind."

Among the Jews, Elias came to be viewed as a precursor to the Messiah and a sign of his coming, a characterization that the Gospels underscore. In Matthew 17: 10-11, the disciples ask Jesus why the scribes say that Elijah (i.e. Elias) must come first, a question to which Jesus responds that "Elijah will indeed come and restore all things." When Jesus asked his disciples, "Who do people say that I am?" the answer was *Some say John the Baptist, others Elijah, still others Jeremiah or one of the prophets*" (Matt. 16: 13-14). Jesus was to many the second Elias. Mt. Carmel, west of Nazareth and within 20 miles of the southern border of Lebanon, was a favorite place of prayer for Saint Elias. As a result, it grew into a great shrine for those devoted to Saint Elias.

The window of Saint Elias represents a protector saint who stands guard against false teachings opposite Saint George. Together they guard the entrance of the church. Saint Elias is portrayed with the golden calf of Baal and stepping on the sword and shield of Baal's followers. The fire represents the fiery chariot that took Saint Elias up into heaven. The sword he holds represents his campaign against the false god Baal and its followers. Saint Elias' feast is July 20.

Saint Rita of Cascia (1381-1457)
Born into a peasant family in Rocca Porrena, Italy, Saint Rita wished at a young age to enter the Augustinian convent in Cascia, Italy. Her parents, otherwise pious folk, wanted her to marry, and when she was eighteen, they pressured her to marry a man who turned out to be impetuous and violent. Saint Rita had two sons with him, and his bad

temper terrorized the whole family. Rita gradually won him over by her piety and patience, but he was nonetheless killed in a brawl with an old enemy. Their sons vowed to avenge their father's death; Rita prayed that they die before they could exact their revenge, and her prayers were answered. Now a widow with no further family responsibilities, she entered the convent in Cascia, where she spent the last 25 years of her life. In the convent, she performed extreme penance. The most famous was her prayer in front of her crucifix asking Jesus to share in his sufferings. A thorn miraculously detached from Christ's crown and embedded itself in her forehead so deeply that the wound festered and became so foul that she was isolated from the other sisters. She suffered in this way for 15 years. When she attended the 1450 Jubilee in Rome, her wound healed, only to reappear after she returned home. As Saint Rita lay dying in 1457, she sent a relative to her old home to get her a rose from the garden. They were out of season, yet her relative found one in full bloom. When she asked for fresh figs—again out of season—they, too were found, ripe and ready to be picked. Her miraculous powers attracted widespread attention, and after her death they continued. As she died, her cell was aglow, and the convent church bell rang by itself. Her body remains incorrupt (i.e. undecayed) to this day. She was canonized in 1900.

The window of Saint Rita portrays her with a rose over her head, signifying the miracle of the rose. In a dish beside her are the miraculous figs. The ray from the crucifix to the thorn in her forehead relates the miracle by which the thorn from her crucifix embedded itself in her forehead. Her feast is May 22.

Saint Theresa of Lisieux (1873-1897)
Theresa Martin was born in Alençon, France, to a prosperous family, the ninth and youngest child, but only the fifth who survived infancy. While she was still very young, Theresa's mother died, and her father moved the family to nearby Lisieux. By most accounts, Theresa even as a child could be difficult: stubborn, nervous, scrupulous, given to black moods and depression, all tendencies she eventually managed to neutralize and control through surrender to God's love. When her sister, Pauline, who acted as a second mother to Theresa, entered the Carmelite convent in Lisieux, Theresa resolved to do the same, and by the age of 14, she was not prepared to wait any longer. Her father

consented, but the superior of the convent opposed the idea. Theresa next took her case to the bishop of Bayeux. He promised he would look into the matter, and encouraged her to make the diocesan pilgrimage to Rome. She did, and in Rome she took her case directly to Pope Leo XIII. At the age of 15, she entered the Carmelite convent, and there developed heroic virtue simply by tending to the little, ordinary, everyday, unspectacular things, and with a spirituality that stressed a profound humility and childlike simplicity, her "Little Way." By so doing, every menial task, every chore became a prayer that sanctified her work and glorified God. In 1894, she contracted tuberculosis, which claimed her life in 1897 at the age of 24. On her deathbed, she promised that "I will let fall a shower of roses—I will spend my heaven doing good upon earth." That has earned her the title of "Little Flower" and her portrayal with roses. While having taken the name of a great activist saint—Saint Theresa of Avila—who came to be recognized as a doctor of the Church, Saint Theresa of Lisieux could not have been more different. But her impact, while quiet, was no less great. She too has been declared a doctor of the church.

She immediately became very popular among the faithful, and was consequently canonized—very quickly for that time—in 1925. Maronite Christians—undoubtedly because of their historically strong ties to France—developed an especially strong devotion to St. Theresa of Lisieux. The Lebanese Mariamite order established the very first church and convent in the world dedicated to Saint Theresa of Lisieux in Sheyleh, region of Kesrowan, Lebanon.

The window of Saint Theresa portrays her with a crucifix, symbol of her great love for Jesus, and with roses, including a rose above her head, signifying her deathbed promise to "let fall a shower of roses." Her feast is October 1.

Saint Ephrem (303-373)
Saint Ephrem was born in Nisibis, Mesopotamia to Christian parents. He befriended Bishop Jacob of Nisibis and his successors, and began to gain an impressive reputation for his talents and eloquence as a gifted teacher, orator, poet, commentator, defender of the Faith and composer of hymns. Saint Ephrem became especially known for his hymns, which he composed to counteract the heresies of the time.

Several heretical sects—the Bardesan heretics among them—put their beliefs to music, which enticed many away from the true Faith, and so Saint Ephrem met the Bardesan challenge by composing hymns on behalf of the Catholic Faith, which won faithful back to the Catholic Faith. In the process, Saint Ephrem awakened the Church to the usefulness of music and poetry, which earned him the title "Harp of the Holy Spirit." Saint Ephrem probably attended the Council of Nicea (which gave us the Nicene Creed) in 325, and he lived in Nisibis during the three Persian sieges, the last of which drove the Christians out. Saint Ephrem then retired to a cave overlooking Edessa, where he lived in austerity and solitude. He left his retreat around 370 to visit Saint Anthony of Egypt and Saint Basil, who ordained him a deacon. During his trip, his ship encountered difficulties, and only through Saint Ephrem's prayers was certain shipwreck averted. In 372 he again left his retreat to assist the people of his region starving during a famine. His efforts for the starving exhausted him, and he died a month after he returned to his cave in 373. Pope Benedict XV declared Saint Ephrem a Doctor of the Church in 1920. His hymns, poems and poetry are in the thousands. Many of the Qolae (plural of Qolo) sung after the Hoosoyo in the Maronite liturgy are attributed to Saint Ephrem's theology and writing, and are consequently known as "Ephrameyat." Saint Ephrem's life attests to his devotion to authentic Christian teaching. He strongly professed the Dogma of the Church, and tirelessly and adamantly opposed all who attacked the Church and its teachings. He dedicated all his life to writing in order to keep the sheep of the Church in the fold and to ward off the wolves from it.

The window of Saint Ephrem depicts him under a grapevine with grapes and also a book. The grape vine represents a common image in Saint Ephrem's writings, especially his commentary on the *Diatessaron* which established parallels or typologies between the Old and New Testaments. Accordingly, the snake in the vine in the garden of Eden led to the harvest of the bitter fruit of sin, and Jesus as the vine of the new covenant (the grapes pressed on the Cross) yields the sweet fruit of salvation. The Aramaic citation in the open book states: " My bones scream from the tomb that the one who gave birth to the Lord is the Blessed Virgin." That represents Saint Ephrem's deep devotion to the Blessed Virgin Mary. Throughout his life he defended the virginity of the Mother of God during the time of the great Christological heresies which questioned her standing in the teachings of the Church. The scroll he holds represents his many dogmatic and ascetic writings. His feast-day falls on January 28.

Saint Anthony the Great, Father of Monasticism (251-356)

Saint Anthony the Great, or Saint Anthony of Egypt, was born at Koman, near Memphis, in Upper Egypt. His parents were wealthy Christians, and after they died, he gave away their money and made sure his sister was cared for. In 272, he became a hermit living in a tomb near Koman. There he lived an austere life of prayer and penance, fasting (he ate only one meal of bread and water each day), manual and intellectual labor and defense of the true Faith. He struggled with numerous temptations; he could have kept his father's money and lived a life of ease instead of being poor and hungry in his hermitage. He faced temptations of the flesh, which he fought by praying to Mary and her Son and by looking at the Cross. So successful was he in his struggles that the devil attacked him directly, beating him and throwing him to the ground. Saint Anthony fought back, but the devil renewed the attack, appearing to him as various wild beasts: snakes, boars and scorpions who stung his body all night long. Saint Anthony bore his sufferings patiently and fought back with fasting, prayer and the Sign of the Cross. In what seems like a reproach, Saint Anthony asked God after his struggles, "Where were you Lord when I was sinking in my blood almost dead?" The point is that Saint Anthony turned to God even during his intense sufferings. The Lord responded, " I was there watching you and enjoying your victory; I will always be with you. I will make great your name in all the earth" (thus Saint Anthony the Great). Owing to his numerous struggles with the devil, Saint Anthony was able to relate with authority that "The devil is very weak, especially when we know how to strip him of his weapons."

Around 285, he sought even greater solitude by establishing his hermitage in an old fortress on Mt. Pispir, where people tossed food over the wall for him. Many sought him out and a community grew around the fortress. In 305, Saint Anthony left his hermitage to establish a monastic community for them—the first ever—in Fayoum, where monks lived separately in solitude, but came together for prayer.

53

In 311 he left his hermitage to encourage the Christians of Alexandria suffering a terrible persecution by the Roman Emperor Maximian. He then moved to a cave near Mt. Kozim. Around 355 Saint Anthony— also a great scholar—again went to Alexandria, to assist his friend, Saint Athanasius, in his struggles against the Arian heresy. During his visit there at the ripe old age of 104, he grabbed the author of the Arian heresy, Arius, by the neck, attempting to straighten out his theological ideas. An ardent activist when he needed to defend the true Faith, Saint Anthony once told the heretics that "You are more poisonous and harmful than serpents." He also indicates what a penance it must have been for him to leave his hermitage to defend authentic Christian teaching: "The hermit without his hermitage is like a fish out of water." Saint Anthony returned from Alexandria to Mt. Kozim, this time for good, and he died there at the age of 105. His monastery still stands; Coptic orthodox monks care for it.

The window of Saint Anthony portrays him with a bell over his head, symbolizing his role as the originator of monasticism, which is especially significant for the Maronite Catholic tradition because it is rooted in monasticism. He holds a book, symbolizing Sacred Scripture and his role in defending Catholic dogma and spreading the teachings of the true Faith. He leans on a Tau cross staff, which he used when he grew tired from standing and praying for hours at a time. He is flanked by tame desert animals who, once intent on hurting him, became his only companions in the desert hermitage. Saint Anthony the Great's feast is January 17.

Saint Rafka (1832-1914)
Saint Rafka—rendered as Rebecca in the Latin Church—was born Boutrossieh Ar-Rayes in Himlaya, near Bifkaya, Lebanon. Her mother died when she was six, and her father remarried, but her relationship with her stepmother became strained and cold. From age eleven to fifteen she worked as a maid, and faced conflicting demands from her stepmother and her aunt over whom she should be promised to in marriage. Boutrossieh informed her family that she chose neither man, and instead wished to enter the convent, a choice her father now rejected. In 1853, when she was 21, she entered the Marian Order of the Immaculate Conception, the Mariamites, a teaching order in

55

Bifkaya, taking the name Anissa. By 1860, her ministry took her to the Shouf region of Lebanon, where she witnessed firsthand the mid-19th-century massacres taking place there, a collaboration of the Ottoman Turks and the local Druze. When Anissa's order reorganized and merged with the Order of the Sacred Heart of Jesus in 1871, she, like all the sisters, was presented the option of remaining in the newly created order or finding another. That same year she joined the Lebanese Maronite Order of Saint Anthony at Saint Simon Convent, in Itoo, Northern Lebanon, taking the new name of Rafka. Her spiritual life deepened here so that she prayed to share in Christ's suffering. Her prayer was answered, and she slowly became blind, accompanied by pain, especially after numerous medical treatments and the surgical removal of one of her eyes, an operation in which she refused anesthesia so that she could offer the pain as a sacrifice to God. All that time, she kept up her community chores as best she could. In 1897 she moved to the convent of Mar-Youssef in Gerabta, and by 1907 she was becoming badly crippled, her body literally disintegrating alive. She now accepted excruciating pain as a gift of God. She lingered in this pain until her death in 1914. God granted her the wish to die near the Sunday of Bartimaeus the Blind Man and the Sunday of the Paralyzed Man, both afflictions with which she was intimately acquainted. Shortly after her death, miracles were reported at her grave. Saint Rafka was beatified in October of 1985, and canonized on June 10, 2001. Saint Rafka is portrayed as a woman who has assumed a role similar to the Blessed Virgin Mary as a suffering mother of sorrows.

The window of Saint Rafka depicts her with a burning lamp over her head, the flame signifying Saint Rafka's ability to see the light of Christ despite the dimming of the light of her own eyesight. It also identifies her as a vigilant wise virgin awaiting her Lord with lighted lamp filled with the oil of faith that never goes dry. She is the patron of the sick, the blind and the crippled. Her feast is March 23.

Saint Sharbel (1828-1898)
Youssef Makhloof was born in Beqa-Kafra in Lebanon, the youngest of five children. His family was a simple, pious farm family that suffered the loss of its father when Youssef was four years old. After his father's death Youssef grew close to his maternal uncles, who were hermits of

the monastery of St. Antonious in Koz-hayah, and when he was 23, he left his village to enter the monastery of Our Lady of Mayfouk in Jebeil. While his family discouraged his desire to be a monk, he craved more seclusion than the monastery in Mayfouk offered. Youssef applied to the Monastery of Saint Maron at Annaya, was admitted to the novitiate in 1851, and took the name Sharbel. Sharbel studied theology at the Monastery at Kfeefan. Blessed Nehmatullah Al-Hardini instructed Theology there and became a powerful spiritual influence on Sharbel. Sharbel was ordained a priest, and returned to Annaya, where he remained for the next 16 years, quickly gaining a reputation for a life of prayer, deep humility, poverty, chastity, devotion and a spirit of obedience. He learned obedience especially well from his hermit uncles and from his saintly mentor, Blessed Nehmatullah Al-Hardini.

Seeking greater perfection still, Sharbel sought more solitude, but his requests to become a hermit were repeatedly denied. However, his superior changed his mind after a miracle occurred. After Sharbel had arrived back to the monastery late from the fields one night, he asked the house servants for some oil for his lamp so he could read his night prayers, despite the fact it was after curfew. The servants decided to play a joke on him and fill the lamp with water instead. He went to his cell, lit the lamp, and read his prayers. Meanwhile, the servants made such a commotion laughing about their joke, that it awakened the superior, who then noticed light coming from Saint Sharbel's cell. Learning of the servants' joke, he realized a miracle had taken place and immediately approved Saint Sharbel's going to the hermitage. Consequently Sharbel entered the nearby Hermitage of Saints Peter and Paul, where he remained for 23 years until his death. Saint Sharbel suffered a stroke in late 1898 while he was celebrating the Divine Liturgy on Christmas Eve, and he died eight days later. His tomb became a pilgrimage site for many, even non-Christians, who saw a great light coming from it. He was exhumed in 1899, four months after his death, and found incorrupt, with blood-like liquid dripping from his body, a phenomenon that continued until the day of his beatification in 1965. Saint Sharbel is known for his many miracles. Between April and July of 1950, 350 miracles at the monastery of Annaya were confirmed, some among Muslims. Saint Sharbel was canonized on October 9, 1977.

The window of Saint Sharbel portrays him with the Cedars of Lebanon, which were near the village of his birth, and he is holding a book, which symbolizes his standing as a great theologian and scholar who meditated day and night on the mystery of Jesus and on Sacred Scripture. Above him is a lamp with a flame, a reminder of the great miracle which made possible his becoming a hermit. His feast is July 23.

Blessed Nehmatullah Al-Hardini (1808-1858)

Youssef Kassab was born to a devout family in Hardeen, Lebanon, the fourth child in a family of six children. Two of the six married; the others all chose lives serving the Church. Youssef entered the Lebanese Maronite Order of monks in 1828, adopting the name Nehmatullah ("Grace of God"). His health was fragile, so he was assigned menial household tasks: laundry, mending, tailoring and bookbinding. In time he became the official tailor and bookbinder of the community. Ordained a priest at the Kfeefan monastery in 1835, he became a gifted professor of moral theology and scholastic philosophy at Kfeefan for the rest of his life. Saint Sharbel Makhloof was one of his students there. He lived an exemplary prayer life, and was especially devoted to the Eucharist, often spending all night in adoration with his hand raised upward as portrayed in the window. His devotion to the Blessed Virgin Mary was similarly fervent. He prayed for the day the dogma of the Immaculate Conception would be formally defined, an event that occurred in 1854, during his lifetime. Strongly committed to fulfilling perfectly his vows of poverty, chastity, and obedience, Blessed Nehmatullah lived a deeply ascetic life, but he did not wish to become a hermit. When his older brother, Elishah, a hermit, tried to get Blessed Nehmatullah to embrace the life of a hermit, Blessed Nehmatullah responded that "Those who struggle for virtue in the life of the community will be granted the greatest merit." By the time he was 37, he was appointed Assistant General of the order, a position he held for three terms, and eventually he was also elected several times to Superior General, but he declined this position each time out of humility. The reason he declined it is because he was unwilling to lord over his fellow brothers: "It is not acceptable for a monk to lead his life in the community as he wishes, but his main concern should be day and night not to hurt or lord it over his brothers." Despite his position as Assistant General, he humbly tended

to his less exalted responsibilities as teacher, tailor and bookbinder. In his later years Blessed Nehmatullah suffered from much ill health, owing in part to his austere life and mortification. After his death, reports of miracles began to circulate, and thus far since his death in 1858, 44 miracles have been documented, many among the Druze and Muslims of Lebanon. Blessed Nehmatullah was beatified on May 10, 1998. Blessed Nehmatullah combined a life of menial labor, occupation with skilled crafts, scholarship, exalted positions with a vibrant spiritual life and deep humility. His saintly life is a marvelous example to our own age of humility and the sanctification of the life of a professional. His admonition that "the wise man is the one who can save his soul" reminds all of what the ultimate priorities should be. Most importantly, Blessed Nehmatullah serves as proof that an active professional and administrator who is not a hermit can still achieve sanctity.

The window of Blessed Nehmatullah depicts him with the host over his head, signifying his great devotion to the Eucharist. Below the host is a book, which reminds us of his role as both a bookbinder and as a teacher. Written in the open book is Blessed Nehmatullah's declaration that "My eyes had dimmed from reading the books." His feast is December 14.

Saint Doumit (died 363)

Saint Doumit was born in Amed, near Mesopotamia, to a pagan family. He eventually ended up in Nisibis, the city of Saint Ephrem, and he became minister to King Wallinz, a client king to the Roman Empire, who was an Arian Christian intent on persecuting Catholic Christians loyal to the apostolic teachings of the Church. Wallinz appointed Doumit to arrest the Catholic Christian leaders of the region in order to torture them and to disperse the faithful. As he was planning his strategy, he was stricken with excruciating pain throughout his body, possibly severe arthritis or Parkinson's Disease. Doumit, screaming from the intense pain, was taken to the royal doctors, who could do nothing for him. Through his intense suffering, he began to realize—much as Saint Paul had done—that he was being punished for his role in persecuting the Catholic Christians. Doumit asked his king to be relieved of his responsibilities and go off to a place of his choice. The

king agreed, and the place he chose was Qurosh (Cyrrhus) Mountain above Antioch, where Saint Maron also would establish a spiritual residence. There, Doumit repented of his sins and lived a hermit's life in a cave, weeping bitterly to atone for his past. He meditated on Sacred Scripture and on the life of Jesus day and night despite his pain, and he was consumed by the joy of the Lord Jesus. There he remained, crippled, for 32 years. Finally he was miraculously cured of his affliction, and God granted him healing powers. The infirm flocked to him to be cured and counseled, and his fame grew. The one-time persecutor of Christians had become a model Christian. Saint Doumit died a martyr's death around 363, a victim of the Roman Emperor Julian the Apostate, who, realizing Doumit had converted to Christianity and turned against him, ordered his execution: "Close that cave door on him and let him die." Churches, monasteries and convents built in his name are numerous in the land of the Maronites.

The window of Saint Doumit portrays him curing a paralyzed beggar. Above his head is an angel, symbol of the Trinity, which Doumit invoked when curing the infirm: "In the name of the Trinity I cure you." It also symbolizes the angel which led him to the faith through his sufferings. Saint Doumit has been characterized as "the brother of the Lord" because of his transformation and elevation through his conversion to Christ. He is the patron of those suffering arthritis, Parkinson's Disease and infirmities of bones and muscles. His feast is August 7, right after the feast of the Transfiguration, a significant placement reflecting Doumit's own spiritual awakening and transformation.

Saint Joseph (1st Century)
Details about the life of Saint Joseph, the foster father of Jesus, are limited to a few passages in the Gospels of Matthew and Luke, and there are no accounts of what he said, earning him the name "the silent saint." But next to the Blessed Virgin Mary and Saint John the Baptist, no saint is more important, since he assumed responsibility for caring for Mary and Jesus. Joseph, whom scripture identifies as "an upright man" descended from the House of David, and his family originated in Bethlehem in Judea, before having moved to Nazareth in Galilee. An upright and just man, Joseph faithfully and unjudgmentally

SAINT JOSEPH

accepted that Mary's unborn child was the work of God, a risk, since according to Jewish law she could have been stoned for being unmarried and with child. He laid aside thoughts of ending his betrothal to Mary, after he understood and accepted God's will conveyed through His messenger who appeared to Joseph in a dream. Thereafter Saint Joseph married Mary and provided for the Holy Family, protecting them from King Herod's persecution by fleeing with Jesus and Mary to Egypt. Joseph lived a life of absolute chastity during his marriage to Mary, and he died a peaceful death before Mary was called to heaven.

The window of Saint Joseph portrays him holding the infant Jesus and a lily, the symbol of his own purity and the Blessed Virgin, whom he cared for as her husband. Above Saint Joseph is a square, the symbol of his occupation as carpenter. He is the patron of family life, a happy death, working people, fathers, and the Universal Church. His feast is March 19.

Blessed Massabki Brothers (martyred July 9, 1860)

The Massabki Brothers—Francis, Abdel Mohti, and Raphael—were Maronites who lived in Damascus, Syria. Francis was a family man with a business; Abdel Mohti was also a family man who gave up a teaching career to become a businessman, until his fears that he might deceive customers led him to a life of meditation. Raphael was a struggling bachelor. All three of them lived lives of exemplary virtue, meditation and piety and were well-respected by both Christians and Muslims in Damascus. On July 9, 1860, Ahmed Pasha, the Muslim ruler of Syria, unleashed a vicious massacre of Christians in Damascus after having fabricated criminal activities the Christians supposedly perpetrated. Even many Muslims did not support Ahmed Pasha's impending response, but their voices were ignored. As remaining Christians fled for safety, Ahmed Pasha's henchmen put Christian churches to the torch, first the Orthodox, and then the Catholic. Many Christians, including the Massabki Brothers, sought refuge at the Franciscan friary chapel. The doors were blockaded, but Ahmed's agents entered through a secret passage shown them by one of the household staff. The house superior, knowing he was about to die, swallowed all the hosts in the tabernacle. That way he would die having

received Jesus, and prevent the desecration of the Eucharist. Ahmed's agents seized the house superior and killed him and all the other religious. Then they presented the laity hiding out there a choice: convert to Islam or die. The Massabki Brothers refused, preferring death over conversion to Islam. One of them explained simply: "I am a Maronite and on the Faith of Christ I will die." All three were brutally killed with knives and hatchets. The Massabki Brothers, who as Christian laity paid with their lives for their devotion to their Maronite Catholic Faith, are especially appropriate models for lay Christians active in the world. Accordingly, they have been made patrons of the lay Apostolate of the Maronite Church in the United States.

The window of the three Massabki brothers shows them facing their death before the altar of the chapel of the Franciscan friary, the Maronite Antiochene cross in the background. Above them is the hand of God reaching down from the cloud (Heaven) to receive their souls, which they commended into God's hands. The Massabki Brothers were beatified in 1926. Their feast is July 10.

Saint Jude (died 68)
Saint Jude, also known as Thaddeus, and in Lebanon as Lebbaeus or Laba, was one of the most well-traveled of the twelve apostles. He was brother of Simon the Zealot (or Canaanite), who eventually became the bishop of Jerusalem, and Saint James the Lesser, and a relative of Jesus. Ancient accounts indicate that he traveled extensively, preaching in Judea, Samaria, Idumaea, Syria, Mesopotamia, Libya, Arabia and Armenia, and that his first mission was to Christianize Beirut in Lebanon. He quite literally covered the four corners of the known world, analogous to the shape of a cross. He is frequently credited with writing an epistle to the churches of the East, which targeted Simonian, Nicolaite and Gnostic heresies.

During his travels to Persia, St. Jude won converts through his gift of prophecy. As Bardakh, the king of Persia, was preparing to invade India, he awaited a sign from his sorcerers in order to begin his attack. St. Jude, however, advised the opposite of what the sorcerers were saying, in the process attempting to discredit their idols and prophecies. The angry sorcerers attempted—ultimately unsuccessfully—to kill him. St. Jude's prophecy that the Persians

could gain a complete victory without war actually came to pass, and so the royal court and the whole kingdom of Persia converted to Christianity. Some sources state that St. Jude suffered martyrdom in Mesopotamia and others identify Armenia as the site of his martyrdom; still others maintain that after his many travels, he returned to Beirut, built a church, and was martyred and buried there. Saint Jude came to be identified as the patron of hopeless cases, possibly because he bore the same name as Judas Iscariot, who betrayed Jesus. As a result, the confusion of names led to a certain amount of neglect among the Christian faithful. St. Jude came to be well known for his humility, his love for Christ, and his preaching and exhortations to the Truth.

The window of Saint Jude portrays him holding a club, the symbol of his martyrdom, and a book, signifying his preaching of the Gospel. The Phoenician ship above his head symbolizes his travels throughout the Mediterranean basin, and the Phoenician design of the ship identifies the Phoenicians—predecessors of the Lebanese—as one of the most important seafaring peoples of the entire Mediterranean world. Just as the Phoenicians tenaciously clung to their false god, Baal, their successors, the Lebanese, clung to the true God and to their Maronite Catholic faith despite numerous and fierce persecutions throughout history. Saint Jude was martyred in 68. His feast is June 19.

Saint Michael the Archangel

Saint Michael's name means "God's Mighty One" and he is one of the three main archangels identified in Scripture, the other two being Gabriel ("Messenger") and Raphael ("God's Merciful One"). Angels are not human, but are of a higher order of being. Like God, they are pure spirits, although unlike God, they are not eternal, since they are creatures created by God, and therefore had a beginning. The Jews regarded Michael in the Old Testament as the special protector of Israel, and Catholic Christianity has come to view him since apostolic times as the protector of the Church. The Greek church fathers and many other theologians have viewed him as the prince over all the seraphim, the highest angelic order of all, and the highest judge over all the other angels. The Book of the Apocalypse describes Saint Michael as the leader of the heavenly angels over the forces of the fallen angels who rejected God, led by the most brilliant angel of all, Lucifer,

also known as Satan. The angels who rejected God were consequently cast into hell as devils.

The window of Saint Michael portrays him as a soldier with a lance piercing a beast, which signifies Satan and evil. His armor identifies his role as guardian of Christians, and the tongue of fire over his head emphasizes his role as spiritual protector against the forces of evil and the guardian of sinners' souls and bodies. The scale above Saint Michael indicates his role as "Scale of Souls," the judge of souls at the hour of death and as the escort of souls to heaven. His feast is September 6.

Saint Takla or Thecla (1st Century)
Saint Takla lived during apostolic times. She converted through the efforts of Saint Paul in Iconium, Lycaonica (modern-day Turkey) around the year 45, and she became an important assistant to Saint Paul. After her baptism she vowed to remain a virgin, ending her betrothal to her intended husband. Her influential parents, embarrassed by her decision, denounced her as a Christian to the authorities, who arrested her and threw her onto a burning pyre. Saint Takla hoped to share in the suffering of Christ on the pyre, but the fire was extinguished by a sudden rainstorm, and she escaped unharmed. She accompanied Paul's group to Antioch, where she served the Christian faithful, and where Paul assigned her the task of converting pagan women there. Her beauty attracted the lustful attentions of a man in Antioch who tried to rape her. She escaped his clutches, but the man, embarrassed at his failure to violate her, turned her in to the governor. Numerous witnesses testified on her behalf, but to no avail. The governor ordered that she be sent to the arena naked, so that all could leer at her while a female lion—the most vicious one on hand— could tear her apart. The lion laid at Saint Takla's feet and a mysterious light clothed her. The following day, she was led back to the arena, now facing several lions. Instead of attacking her, one lion sat by her to protect her, and another laid down in veneration at her feet, licking them. Then she was bound to four bulls who were to be driven in opposite directions; she would have been torn apart had the bulls not refused to move. The bulls instead gored her executioners. Finally she was thrown into a snake pit, but a lightning bolt killed the snakes before she could be harmed. Saint Takla was then freed. She met up with Paul again at Marylykia before returning to Iconium to spread the

Gospel in her homeland. Her fiancé was dead but her mother was not—and she was still very angry. Saint Takla headed instead to the mountains of Lebanon and lived a prayerful life as a hermit in a cave in the mountains of the Qualamoun and Chekka regions. From here, Saint Takla helped to Christianize northern Lebanon, and Maaloula and Seydnaya in Syria. Meanwhile, she became so famous for her cures that she put all the local doctors out of business. They hatched a plot to kill her, which she dismissed as trivial after all the plots she had already survived. She died peacefully at 90 years of age, and was buried in Seleucia, southwest of Antioch. Saint Takla is known as the first woman to face martyrdom for her Christian faith—even though all attempts to kill her actually failed. In that sense, her longevity itself is a miracle.

The window of Saint Takla portrays her wearing the martyr's crown of roses, which also signifies her purity. She is depicted in the arena with the two lions, and above her head are two symbols of martyrdom, the flame and the palm. She is especially celebrated in the areas where she was active. Her feast is September 24.

Saint Stephen (1st Century)

Most of what we know about Saint Stephen comes from the Acts of the Apostles. He was a Greek-speaking Jew of the Diaspora, and after conversion by Saint Peter, he became a devoted Christian. He was one of the original seven deacons the apostles ordained to assist in the growing administrative responsibilities of the Christian sect. Because of his zeal, honesty and dedication, the apostles appointed him the head of the deacons, or proto-deacon, where all who came into contact with him experienced that he was filled with Faith, strength, grace and the Holy Spirit. He served as the most important assistant to the disciples, preaching, distributing the Eucharist, protecting church property and organizing almsgiving on behalf of the poor. St. Stephen was also a talented and effective defender of the Christian Faith. He silenced all his opponents, whether they were Cyrenian, Alexandrian or Cilician Jews, and one of their best scholars observed how well "the wisdom of this man stands before the wisdom of God." Since St. Stephen had been a highly respected Jew, his colleagues felt betrayed by his vigorous preaching that Jesus was the long-awaited Messiah. His miracle-working and his preaching of the Christian faith led to his denunciation to the Jewish authorities, the Sanhedrin, which charged him with blasphemy, a crime punishable by death. He courageously defended the Christian faith, explaining how Jesus was the Messiah promised throughout Jewish scripture and tradition. He concluded by blasting his accusers:

> You stiff-necked people, uncircumcised in heart and ears, you are always opposing the Holy Spirit just as your fathers did before you. Was there any prophet whom your fathers did not persecute? In their day they put to death those who foretold the coming of the Just One; now you in your turn have become his betrayers and murderers. You who received the law through the angels have not observed it. (Acts 7: 51-53)

St. Stephen's spirited defense of the Christian Faith infuriated the Sanhedrin, who, having long sought ways to silence him, judged him guilty of blasphemy and ordered him dragged outside of Jerusalem and stoned to death. As powerfully as he had defended the Gospels of Jesus, he surrendered himself like a lamb to his executioners. While he was being stoned, he forgave his persecutors: "Lord, do not hold this sin against them" (Acts 7: 60). One of the participants in St. Stephen's execution was a man named Saul (the man we later know as St. Paul), who fanatically rejected Christianity as a blasphemous aberration from Judaism. He encouraged Stephen's persecutors as they stoned him, and held their cloaks for them. The Lord had heard St. Stephen's final plea, for Saul the executioner himself later converted, and went on to become the apostle to the nations, effectively continuing the mission of Saint Stephen.

In 415, during the reign of Arkadius, son of Theodosius the Great, a priest named Lukianos discovered the tombs of St. Stephen, Gamaliel (Paul's teacher) and Nicodemus outside Jerusalem. He exhumed them, and brought their relics with great ceremony to Jerusalem. The relics of St. Stephen became famous for thousands of cures among the terminally ill.

The window of Saint Stephen depicts him dressed as a deacon. The stones symbolize the means of his death. The palm in his hand is the martyr's symbol. Saul stands in the background, holding a red cloak. Saint Stephen's feast is December 27.

Conclusion

We hope that this "Colorful Bouquet Of Saints" has shed some light on these saints and brought you a clearer understanding of their exemplary lives. It is important to note that the saints whose lives are briefly narrated in this book are not being categorized or labeled as "Eastern" or "Western.." A canonized saint belongs no longer to his or her particular Church but to the entire flock of the One Shepherd and Lord Jesus Christ.

Part II showed the origin of the Catholic Church and listed various traditions of East and West, which branched out from its early history. The list of these particular churches helps us all as Catholics to better understand various backgrounds of the Universal Church and enables us to trace the origin of our own particular tradition. Part III was not intended to discuss the glorious history of the Maronite Church. We felt the need to provide Maronites with a deeper understanding of their own tradition and non-Maronites with a detailed definition of the origin and the identity of the Maronite Church. A succinct summary, in eight major characteristics, was provided to the reader in order to appreciate the intricate origin and the complex identity of this rich and valued tradition.

We hope that through this book we have provided you with greater insights about the church renovation, and a fuller explanation of its new artwork and stained glass. The church renovations present and reflect continuity with the Maronite heritage we share with our ancestors and forefathers. We further hope that the explanation of the art and the lives of the saints will give you a fuller appreciation of the antiquity and depth of the Maronite tradition, and of the rich Maronite spiritual heritage that has so greatly inspired the Universal Church. We would like to conclude by joining our prayers with the prayers of the Maronite priest as he concludes the Qurbono (Mass) saying: "…Guard me, O Lord, and protect your holy Church, that she may be the way to salvation and the light of the World. Amen."

Exemplary
Contributors

Exemplary Contributors

A word of gratitude is due to those parishioners whose exemplary generosity has greatly contributed to the completion of the renovation project and to the beautification of our Church in preparation for the centennial of our parish.

Stained Glass Windows

St. George	Jacques and Renee Khangi
St. Elias	Sally Moran and Family
St. Rita	Tony and Rima Zinaty
St. Theresa	Gabriel and Marie Chouchani
	Adel and Yasmine Chouchani
St. Ephrem	Naim and Rima Dawli
St. Anthony the Great	The Family of John Chameli
St. Rafka	Richard and Rosemary Saffire
St. Sharbel	Bertha Hayek
Blessed Nehmatullah	Arthur and Reina Joseph
	Darlene DiFrancesco
St. Doumit	Assad and Marilyn Shady
	Joseph and Antoinette Shehadi
	Doumit and Georgette Shady
St. Joseph	Jeanette Lombardo
	Joseph Lombardo
Blessed Massabki Brothers	Michael and Victoria Karam
St. Jude	The Family of Elias and Rose Attea
St. Michael	The Dewan Family
St. Takla	Farid Abou Jaoude and Family
St. Stephen	Fouad and Sonia Badawy

Exemplary Contributors

Stained Glass Transoms

The Papal and the Patriarchal
Coats of Arms

Roger and Sylvia Jammal

Qadeesha, or The Holy Valley

Joseph and Yvette Shehadi
Michael and Sandra Shehadi

Our Lady of Lebanon

Richard and Nouhad Boorady
Edward and Ethel Boorady
Frederick and Marilyn Boorady
Edna Boorady
Robert Boorady

Murals

St. Maron

David and Joan Marie Deinhart
Joseph and Theresa Bittar

The Blessed Mother

Mansour Chayban and Family

The Antiochene Cross &
the Centerpiece

Mary Lee Elias

St. John the Beloved Disciple

Magid Mansour and Family

St. John Maron

Richard and Hariette Attea

Special thanks as well to the many anonymous parishioners and individuals who generously donated Time, Talent and Treasure toward our Church renovation project.

Generous Sponsors

In Loving Memory
Of

Marie & Antoine Habib

Saide & Norman Joseph

Bedie Norman Joseph

Amelia Marie Moran

Mamie Marie Moran

Thank You For Teaching Us To Love And To Serve

The Needs Of Others And To Appreciate

Our Maronite Heritage And Lebanese Culture

Amy & Halim A. Habib
& Family

IN LOVING MEMORY OF

OUR GRANDPARENTS

HELEN & JOSEPH (GUISH) MOSEY

IN LOVING MEMORY

OF

MY GODMOTHER

JEANETTE ANNE WILLIAMS

Respectfully

By Russell Sharbel Williams & Family

In Honor Of Our Mother

Jeanette Daniel-Lombardo

Thank You for Instilling In Us
The Spirit of Serving Others And
The Love of Our Maronite Tradition

Jeanette Lombardo-Thomas
Jerome Lombardo
Joseph Lombardo

In Loving Memory

Of

Georgette & Joseph Attea

COURTESY
OF
DELFT PRINTING

Mr. & Mrs. Kamal Aboujaoude

IN LOVING MEMORY
OF THE
MICHAEL

& THE
# TARTAK

FAMILIES

NOTES

NOTES